Learn to Swim the Australian Way
Level 3 Intermediate
Written by AlyT

Learn To Swim the Australian Way
Level 3 Intermediate

Part of the Learn to Swim the Australian Way series with AlyT

DEDICATED TO

my mother **RHONDA** aka **MRS PAUL** who taught me everything I needed to know about life & Jesus ✝

AND my mentor **PETER TIBBS** aka **TIBBSIE**; both of whom helped mould me into the swimmer and swimming teacher I am today.

Written by AlyT
© Copyright 2022 by Allison Tyson
All rights reserved. No part of this book may be used or reproduced in any manner whatsoever, including photocopying, social media platforms and/or other electronic or mechanical methods, without written permission of the publisher.
For more information write: Aly T, PO Box 6699, Cairns City, QLD 4870.

Formatting: Aluycia Suceng
Editing : Phoenix Raig
Illustrator: PicassoJR
First printing: 2022

Disclaimer
While we draw on our own prior professional expertise and background in the area of teaching learn to swim, by purchasing and reading our products you acknowledge that we have produced this book for informational and educational purposes only. You alone are solely responsible, and take full responsibility for your own wellbeing as well as the health, lives and wellbeing of your family and children in your care.

www.borntoswim.com.au
SwimMechanics@yahoo.com
Other books by this Author include:
Water Awareness Newborns
Water Awareness Babies
Water Awareness Toddlers
Learn to Swim the Australian Way Level 1 – The Foundations
Learn to Swim the Australian Way Level 2 – The Basics

SAFETY FIRST!

* NEVER SWIM ALONE

The non-swimmer should always be accompanied by a responsible adult who can swim. Where possible, let the lifeguard on duty know you are learning to swim or a beginner swimmer. ALWAYS stay within arm's reach of young and beginner swimmers.

* NEVER FORCE A SWIMMER UNDER THE WATER

Learning to swim should be fun & appropriate to the individual's pace. Be mindful of how you hold and help a swimmer as they learn; repeat cues and demonstrate skills as much as you can, and never use force.

* NEVER HOLD YOUR BREATH FOR EXTENDED PERIODS OF TIME

Hyperventilating and breath holding games are dangerous and can cause you to faint (lose consciousness) in the water (search shallow water black-out). Exchanging CO_2 and Oxygen via blowing bubbles is extremely important when swimming to avoid fatigue and to help the swimmer stay balanced.

* LEARNING TO SWIM IN SHALLOW, WAIST DEPTH WATER IS BEST FOR BEGINNERS

Until you can confidently move yourself through the water and float comfortably on your back, beginner swimmers should continue to practise in shallow water only.

A NOTE TO ALL THE THE MERMAIDS & AQUAMEN LEARNING TO SWIM,

Welcome to **LEARN TO SWIM THE AUSTRALIAN WAY: INTERMEDIATE.**

CONGRATULATIONS on completing the 21 skills from Level 2 — The Basics! You now know how to move safely on your back, balance vertically, exhale under the water, coordinate your arm movements with your legs and perform a variety of floats and kicking techniques. Most importantly, you've also learnt **HOW TO BE SAFER AND MORE CONFIDENT** around water. Are you ready to have even more fun learning to swim?

Just as in our first two books, in Level 3 we'll uncover **21 NEW SKILLS** to help **BUILD MUSCLE MEMORY, IMPROVE BALANCE AND INCREASE TRACTION & PROPULSION** in the water. Now it's time to **EXPAND OUR SWIMMING KNOWLEDGE** and move onto new challenges with our goal of **MASTERING THE PREPARATION** for the four competitive strokes **(FREESTYLE, BACKSTROKE, BREASTSTROKE AND BUTTERFLY)**, make improvements to our dives, and work on our turns and starts. We'll also learn some more **FUN WATER SAFETY STUFF** too.

For the parents and teachers who will be assisting with these skills, ensure your **SWIM STUDENT PERFORMS EACH SKILL**, to the best of their ability, **4-5 TIMES EVERY LESSON. DON'T BE AFRAID TO CORRECT MISTAKES AND ALWAYS GIVE LOTS OF PRAISE AND ENCOURAGEMENT**. For our student swimmers, remember that 'I can't' doesn't exist in the learner swimmer's vocabulary, but **'I'LL TRY' AND A BIT OF EFFORT** always should. Some skills you'll learn in minutes, others may take weeks and months of hard work. Aim to **ISOLATE, POLISH AND REFINE EACH OF THE SWIMMING SKILLS AT EVERY LESSON**. Small adjustments of body positioning and use of the **VERBAL CUES** will fast track learning and memory recall.

We have organised the 21 skills for our swimmers to **GRADUALLY PROGRESS** in a way that **DEVELOPMENTALLY MAKES SENSE**; moving to the next skill before you've properly mastered the current ones, skipping past a skill and the continual practise of a skill with poor form, with no regard to correct body positioning, will lead to bad habits and sloppy swimming.

To **ACCELERATE LEARNING**, always practise new skills over **SHORT DISTANCES OF 2-3 METERS IN SHALLOW WATER**; practising newly learnt skills over long distances leads to fatigue and the new skills and technique will tend to fall apart.

Once again, for ease of learning, we've included **VISUAL CUES, CATCHY NAMES** and easy to remember **VERBAL CUES** for each of the skills. All learner swimmers, teachers and parents should remember to follow the motto **'LEARN SLOW TO SWIM FAST'**, and adhere to the four P's of learning: **PATIENCE, PRAISE, PERFECTION AND PRACTICE**.

Yours swimmingly,

Alyt

PS The fastest way to improve your swimming is to **GET IN THE WATER AND PRACTISE OFTEN**, at least three times a week. See you at the next level!

I CAN DO A COMPACT JUMP ENTRY!

I never enter the water without an adult who can swim.

Before jumping into the water, I first check:
1. the depth of the water?
2. is there a safe place for me to get in and out of the water?
3. is someone close by paying attention, watching to help me if I need them?

Brace and lock

WARNING — SHUT THE GATE

A Compact Jump should be used when I am jumping into deep water from a height, like from a pier or a boat during an emergency. In real life situations, when around open water and in boats or other recreational water vehicles, it's important to wear a lifejacket, also known as a Personal Floatation Device (PFD). This will keep me safe if I accidentally fall or have to go in the water.

To practice my Compact Jump, I move to deeper water and stand on the side of the pool with my toes curled over the edge. I squeeze my nose and cover my mouth with one hand, resting my bent arm across my chest. I then cross my other arm over the top, firmly grasping my opposite shoulder, squeezing against the first arm to lock the hand holding my nose and mouth in place. If I am wearing a lifejacket, I use the hand NOT holding my nose to hold onto the neck of the PFD to stop it from lifting over my head as I jump into the water.

As I step out into the deep water, away from the pool deck, I straighten my legs and point my toes keeping my feet together. I continue to brace and lock my nose as I enter the water toes first. I can also try a Compact Jump with my knees bent and tucked under me. As I enter, my feet are flat to absorb the shock of hitting the water. After I jump in, I always return to safety or float and wait for help.

I CAN SIDE BREATHE!

1 I practise breathing to the side by either sitting in shallow water with a kickboard, or standing and holding onto the side of the pool. To keep myself steady I put one hand on my knee and reach my other arm forward, locking my elbow to keep the arm straight and in line with my shoulder.

2 I take in a Pufferfish Breath, place my face into the water with my ear pressed against my reaching arm, and look straight down as I count 1-2-3 in my head and blow lots of bubbles.

3 My arms and body stay very still, as I learn to only turn my head when I need to breathe. If I press my ear into the water as I turn to breathe, it reminds me not to lift my face out or look forwards when taking a breath.

4 After a quick breath in, I turn my face back into the water, look straight down and start to blow my bubbles as I count to three again.

BUBBLES!

Eyes down

BREATHE!

Ear in the water

I do lots of practice, taking time to learn to breathe to my left and to my right.

I CAN CANOE FLOAT & KICK!

To Canoe Float, I lean my upper back into the water as I gently push off the bottom of the pool with both feet. I look straight up and relax my head into the water, letting it cover my ears and surround my face. I keep my arms straight and my hands resting on my upper thighs as I point my feet away and turn my toes inwards, keeping them just below the surface.

At first, I practise my Canoe Float and Kicks with a kickboard to help round out my shoulders and put me in the correct body position for Backstroke. I Crocodile Hold the kickboard over the top of my legs, keeping my hands close together in the middle of the kickboard. My shoulders roll in as I keep my arms straight, reaching towards my legs as I kick. While kicking, I press my hips against the board to keep my back flat and head steady, looking straight up.

I kick hard and fast – I'll need a strong kick for when I learn Backstroke. My legs always stay long and my ankles loose as I kick. My knees bend only slightly, but if they start hitting the kickboard, I soften my kick and straighten my legs.

Toes under

Hips up

No knees

Ears under

Once I can kick smoothly, I practise my Canoe Float & Kicks without a kickboard by resting my hands on my upper thighs and reaching forwards without lifting my head or ears out of the water.

It is important someone stays behind me when I float and kick on my back so I don't hit my head on the side of the pool or run into another swimmer.

I CAN MISSILE FLOAT!

Heels together

I lean into the water, with my arms reaching forwards squeezed against my ears as I look straight down. My hands are flat, with my palms facing the bottom of the pool and my thumbs touching. My body stays straight, taut not tense, as I stretch myself forward by pressing my armpits into the water, pointing my feet behind me and bringing my big toes together so they are touching for the count of 1-2!

Now I am ready to practise Blasting Off and gliding across the water in the Missile Float position.

I Blast Off, staying balanced in my Missile Float for the count of 1-2! As I begin to slow down, I relax my legs and bend my knees, drawing my feet up behind me into a Frog Float. I balance again in a Missile Frog Float for the count of 1-2-3!

Find your toes

Stretch & press

Thumbs together

The Missile Float will help me glide through the water when I learn to Breaststroke.

I CAN DO ANGEL WING SWINGS!

> I can practise my Angel Wing Swings on the pool deck, standing against a wall, or in shallow water. Learning to swing my arms will help me remember how my arms need to move when I learn to swim Butterfly.

Thumbs at sides

Palms out

SWING!

Elbows High

PUSH!

1 I start with relaxed hands dangling at my sides, thumbs touching my thighs. With my eyes looking straight ahead I exhale and swing both my arms out and up.

2 As I lift and swing my arms, I keep them straight and lead my Angel Wing Swings with the back of my wrists until my arms are in line with my shoulders over my head. I pause here for a moment, pointing my fingertips towards the sky, palms turned outwards in a standing Fly Float position.

3 I breathe in and bend my arms forwards, poking my elbows out to the sides and press my palms towards the ground. My hands move down and in towards my belly button then back out again, thumbs brushing my sides as I blow another breath out and begin the next swing.

I CAN BACKSTROKE MARCH!

I Backstroke March on the pool deck or in shallow water to help me move my feet and swing my arms backwards at the same time for when I learn to swim Backstroke.

Straight arm lift

LIFT!

PRESS!

Push to my side

I hold the kickboard in front of me with both hands close together using a firm Crocodile Hold. Then I let go with one hand.

My elbow is locked to keep my arm straight. As I lift, I lead with my wrist and my hand stays relaxed with loose fingers.

As my arm shaves past my ear and reaches behind me, I turn my hand so my palm is facing outwards and press my hand and straight arm towards the side of my leg to grab the kickboard.

My arm holding the kickboard must stay straight and not move as I lift and press with each arm. I practice breathing in as I lift and breathing out as I press.

I CAN DO RAINBOW ARMS!

The kickboard will remind me:
1. to keep my arms straight and extended forwards
2. to maintain a firm grip as I hold the kickboard
3. to return my hand to the correct place when I finish each stroke

I use a kickboard to build up my stamina and to perfect my Rainbow Arms so that I can swim Freestyle.

REACH!

I start by taking in a Pufferfish Breath and Crocodile Hold the kickboard with both hands. I look straight down and Blast Off smoothly across the surface of the water, kicking lots of fast little kicks. I reach forwards with the kickboard, remembering to keep my arms straight and pressed against my ears.

PULL!

As I blow my bubbles, I begin my Rainbow Arms by letting go of the kickboard with one hand and sweeping it under me, down past the side of my leg. When my thumb brushes past my leg, I lift my arm out of the water, elbow first, using my shoulder for a big arm swing, like a rainbow arching over the water. My Rainbow Arm has a soft relaxed hand as I paint the sky with my trailing fingertips. My wrist leads as my arm comes over the water and shaves past my ear to grab the kickboard – fingertips first.

SWING!

I try to do two slow Rainbow Arms, one after the other, without having to take a breath. When I am ready, I try to do four slow Rainbow Arms exhaling long, slow bubbles. I stop, stand up and rest when it is time to take a breath, then it is time to try another four Rainbow Arms.

I CAN DO BUBBLE ARM BREATHING ARM!

> Bubble Arm Breathing Arm helps me remember to breathe when I move one arm and blow bubbles when I move the other.

BREATHING ARM

Ear in the water

BUBBLE ARM

Eyes down

I practise by sitting in shallow water and Crocodile Holding a kickboard with both hands. I take in a Pufferfish Breath and press my face into the water between my outstretched arms. My Breathing Arm stays straight and locked in place holding the kickboard as I blow bubbles, sweeping my Bubble Arm down to my leg and arching it over the water to grab the kickboard.

I swap arms when my Bubble Arm reaches the kickboard and immediately begin to press the water behind me with my Breathing Arm.

I take in a quick breath by turning my head to the side after my Breathing Arm has let go of the kickboard. I turn my head back into the water after my thumb touches my leg and my arm starts to swing over the water. I make sure my face is back in the water before my hand reaches for the kickboard.

It is important I don't lift my head or roll on my back when I take a breath; pressing my ear and cheek into the water and keeping my Bubble Arm straight and taut will help me stay balanced as I turn to breathe. I also practise swapping my Breathing Arms so I can become good at breathing to the left and the right.

When I am ready, I can go for a swim bubbling and breathing as I kick with a kickboard.

I CAN DO A BLAST OFF ON MY BACK!

I start by moving to deeper water and holding onto the wall of the pool. I lift myself forward towards the side of the pool and walk my feet up the pool wall. As I crouch against the wall, my arms stay bent and shoulder width apart. My hands and arms carry my weight as I keep my knees directly under my armpits, tucking my elbows in as I tilt my head back towards the water.

I blow Dragon Bubbles when I Blast Off on my back to stop the water from sneaking up my nose. I practice many times to see how far and how smoothly I can glide over the water, rolling over and kicking back to safety each time I complete a successful Blast Off.

WARNING
SHUT the GATE

With my ears under the water and eyes looking straight up, I count down 3-2-1 and Blast Off pushing myself backwards from the wall using my toes and the balls of my feet. To add even more rocket power, I use my hands to push the water towards my toes by extending and stretching my arms down to my legs and resting my hands on my thighs.

1.6 m

Toes under

Hips up

Ears Under

I CAN DO A SWORDFISH START & ROTISSERIE ROLL!

Like a Blast Off, a Swordfish Start prepares me to take off from the wall, but on my side. I practise my Swordfish Starts very slowly until I can do them super-fast.

I hold onto the wall of the pool with one arm behind me whilst I look in the direction I want to go. My lead arm stays locked out in front of me, helping me balance. My knees are bent and my feet are pressed against the wall of the pool.

When I am ready, I take a deep breath and turn my head to the side, pressing my ear against my lead arm. My arm grasping the wall behind me lets go and arches over the water to join my lead arm as I drop under the water. Before I Blast Off, I lock my hands together with my thumbs, squeeze my ears with my arms and push off the wall using the balls of my feet and my toes. I Torpedo Stretch off the wall and shoot through the water, exhaling a long stream of bubbles as I glide towards the surface.

Once I have perfected my Swordfish Start and am able to keep my Torpedo Stretch locked as I glide, I practise taking off and rolling from my side to my front or my back. I do this by performing a Rotisserie Roll. A Rotisserie Roll helps me learn to get comfortable on my back, looking up at the surface as I glide under the water, using my upper body to turn me over and direct me towards the surface.

ROLL

Torpedo locked

I CAN MERMAID UNDERWATER!

Now that I know how to Caterpillar Kick, I can start to Mermaid Underwater.

Hip press

To Mermaid, I Blast Off under the water with my arms by my sides. As I glide, I dip my chest forwards and bend my knees slightly, kicking downwards with both feet. As I kick down the front of my feet press against the pressure of the water so my bottom lifts upwards and my body arches like a dolphin. I draw my feet up quickly by bending my knees slightly and raising my feet together behind me, ready to give another soft dolphin-like kick.

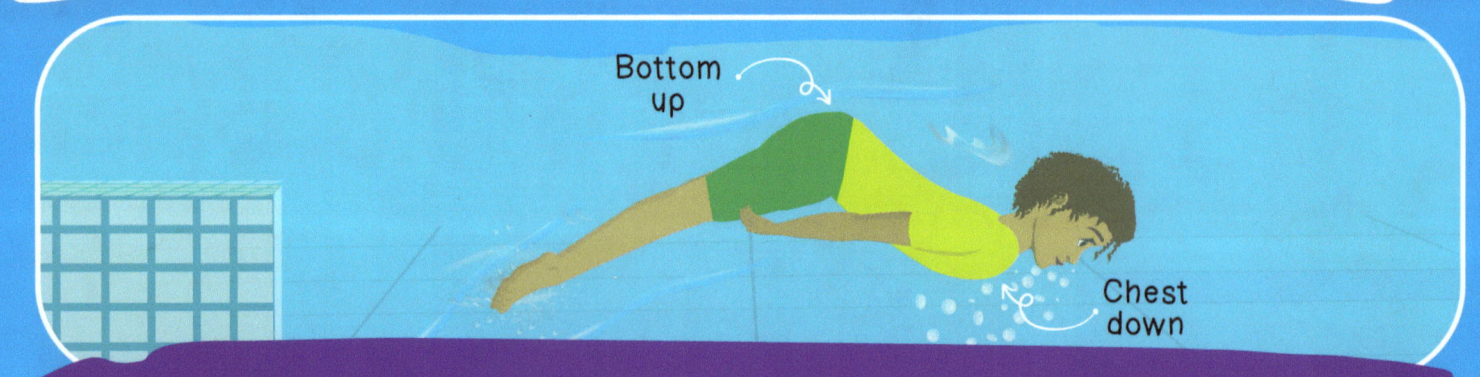

Bottom up

Chest down

I do three gentle soft kicks, letting my body rise and fall across the bottom of the pool before I come up to take a breath. I also practice Mermaiding on my side and on my back.

I CAN BODY DOLPHIN!

Toe flick

I Blast Off gently from the side of the pool with my arms extended, thumbs down in a Fly Float. I press my chest forwards so my hips rise out of the water when my feet kick downwards and together; being mindful not to leave my feet hanging down for too long before drawing them up quickly to start my upkick.

When I upkick, I don't bend my knees too much behind me. I keep my feet and the rest of my body just under the water's surface with only my toes sneaking a peek, breaking through the water's surface to give a small toe flick at the start of each dolphin-like kick.

Hips up

Chest press

As I Body Dolphin, I blow a continuous stream of bubbles and reach forwards with my arms. I imagine I am kicking over and under small waves in the ocean like a dolphin. I do three gentle Body Dolphins then I stop and have a rest to catch my breath.

I CAN DO A TORPEDO STREAMLINE!

To Torpedo Streamline I start at the pool wall using a Swordfish Start. As I launch, I extend into a submerged Torpedo Stretch followed by three Body Dolphins.

TORPEDO LOCKED

To maintain my speed, it is important my hands stay locked when I Body Dolphin by using my thumbs to clasp my hands together. My arms squeeze the backs of my ears as I look straight down and stretch out as long as I can as I push off on my side.

I experiment with three long, slow Body Dolphins and three super-fast Body Dolphins to gauge which Torpedo Streamline sends me faster and the furthest under the water.

I CAN DO SIX KICKS LIFT & PUSH!

Now that I know how to Backstroke March and Canoe Float & Kick on my back, I am ready to start coordinating my arms and legs in the water for Backstroke. I can practise Six Kicks Lift & Push with and without a kickboard.

It's a good idea to have someone behind me to help me swim straight and not bump my head on the wall of the pool or run into other swimmers.

Ears Under

Straight arm lift

Press to my thigh

1 I Blast Off gently from the wall on my back looking straight up, keeping my ears under the water and my hands reaching forwards, palms down on my upper thighs while I kick fast little kicks.

2 Once my body is balanced, I lift one arm up and over my head, whilst doing six fast kicks. My elbow stays locked and my hand is relaxed as I lift my arm leading with the back of my wrist. My opposite shoulder rolls up and out of the water as my lifting arm shaves past my ear and reaches into the water.

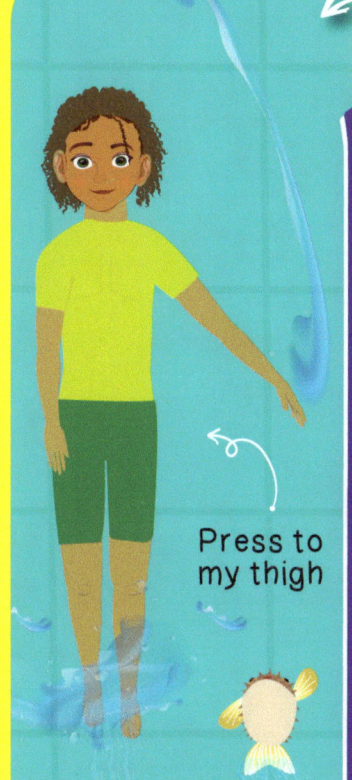

3 Once my hand enters the water, pinky first, I do another six fast kicks as I turn my palm outwards towards the side of the pool and use my whole arm to push the water to my thigh. I kick another six fast kicks as I begin to straight-arm lift and push with my other arm.

I CAN DO A FROG LEGS SEQUENCE!

1 FROG

I Missile Float on a submerged step, or lay on the pool deck, as I relax my feet and bend my legs to draw my feet up behind me. I turn my feet out with my heels together so I am Frog Floating.

2 STARFISH

I then separate my feet, pushing out and around with my heels until my legs are in a Starfish Float with my feet and toes pointed.

3 SNAP

Next, I snap my legs and feet together making sure my big toes touch. Once my big toes are touching and my feet are turned in, I stretch out long and count 1... 2... before starting the sequence again.

> I practise Frog Legs Sequence for when I learn to do Breaststroke. Learning to turn my feet out and push with the soles of my feet can be difficult, so I practise my sequence very slowly until I get it right.

> I move through each float slowly, always pausing for the count of two, after I snap my legs together to find and point my big toes. I take a quick breath and restart after each Frog Legs Sequence.

I CAN DO A FROG ARMS SEQUENCE!

Thumbs down

Y!

Thumbs up

SCOOP!

Thumbs up

SHOOT!

To practise my Frog Arms Sequence for Breaststroke, I lay down and lean over the side of the pool

I start with my face in the water looking down, blowing bubbles. My arms are slightly wider than shoulder width apart so they look like a 'Y', my palms are facing out with my thumbs turned downwards.

Next, I bend my arms and as I push the water towards my chest, I raise myself up, out of the water to take in a breath. This position is called 'Scoop'.

Once my hands come in under my chin, almost touching my chest, I turn my hands over into a prayer-like position. My thumbs are up ready to 'shoot' my hands forwards – up and over the water as fast as I can.

As I 'shoot', I extend my arms forwards and press my armpits into the water, flattening my hands, palms down into the Missile Float position, whilst pressing my face back into the water and blowing bubbles.

I move my arms and upper body from each position Y-SCOOP-SHOOT like I am slowly winding up a crank. I look like a cobra ready to strike just before I 'shoot' my hands forwards as fast as I can to pause in my Missile Float position for the count of 1...2...!

16

I CAN DO SLOW MOTION BUTTERFLY

Now that I can Body Dolphin and Angel Wing Swing, I can begin to learn my Butterfly Arm Sequence by performing Slow Motion Butterfly.

1 FLY FLOAT

2 PULL

3 DEAD FLY FLOAT

4 SWING

5 FLY FLOAT

I start in a Fly Float, with my thumbs turned down, and slowly bend my arms under me to push the water to my belly button, then out to the sides of my legs into a Dead Fly Float.

Once my thumbs have grazed past my thighs, I exhale and slowly swing my arms out of the water and around the sides of my body; leading with the back of my wrists, thumbs trailing just over the top of the water to softly land in a Fly Float.

BODY DOLPHIN

As I Fly Float, I press my chest into the water and do one slow Body Dolphin pushing my fingertips forwards just under the surface of the water. I stand to take a breath, then repeat another Slow Motion Butterfly. I get a little faster and stronger every try until I can do two or three Slow Motion Butterflies at a time.

I CAN DO UNDERWATER TUMBLES!

Underwater Tumbles are fun to learn, but I must be careful not to do them near a wall or in water that is too shallow. I also want to make sure I am not too close to other people – I don't want to risk hitting my head on anyone or tumbling on top of them.

I also need to remember to take a breath before I tumble, and always blow Dragon Bubbles as I turn upside down; otherwise, water will go up my nose, which can hurt or cause me to start sneezing.

To Underwater Tumble on my front, I use the momentum of my Blast Off and my outstretched arms to reach forwards and push water behind me as I bury my head towards my chest and tuck my knees in tight towards my belly. As I flip over, my body looks like a ball spinning under the water.

To Underwater Tumble on my back, I use the momentum of my Blast Off to shoot across the water. Before I start to slow down, I tip my head backward and arch my back to drive myself under the water. I use my arms and Dragon Bubbles to spin myself around backwards like a wheel.

I practise my tumbles until I can spin and land on my feet

Knees tucked

Push with my arms

I CAN TREAD WATER & EGGBEATER KICK!

Treading water using an Eggbeater Kick to keep my face out of the water is an important part of survival swimming. It is useful if I accidentally fall in the water or if I am swimming in deep water and need to stop to have a look around.

I start by practising in shoulder deep water, where I can still touch the bottom of the pool. I tilt my head back slightly and move my hands and forearms in a figure 8 sculling motion under the water.

1.6 m

Chin up

Firm hands

Peddle legs

While my arms and hands continue to move, I lift my feet off the bottom of the pool and bend my knees so that it looks like I am sitting in an imaginary chair while I peddle an imaginary bike with my legs. My legs make large circles under me, this is called an Eggbeater Kick.

When I am ready, I move to deeper water with an adult who can swim and I practise Treading Water holding a pool noodle. I do lots of Seahorse Balances before I try to Tread Water on my own without assistance.

I CAN DO A CROUCH DIVE!

Before practising my Crouch Dive, I move to deeper water – but always with an adult who can swim.

I stand on the edge of the pool and bend my knees, doing a low Bunny Crouch. My knees act as a wound up spring for when I push off with my feet and dive in.

WARNING SHUT the GATE

EYES DOWN!

1.6 m

To prepare for the dive, I lock my hands and pretend to glue my arms to the sides of my head. It is important my arms and hands stay locked as I lean forward and my fingertips point to where I want to land in the water. If my head becomes unglued from my locked arms or my eyes look upwards instead of straight down when I dive in, I will belly flop and water will go up my nose. Squeezing the back of my ears with my arms will help keep my arms in place and remind me to keep my eyes down.

When I am ready to dive, I take in a Pufferfish Breath, look down and hum as I lean forward and spring out from the side of the pool using my toes and the balls of my feet. As I dive in, I follow my hands into the water and straighten my legs out behind me, entering the water in one smooth, arching line. Once under the water, I maintain my speed by using a Torpedo Streamline to the surface.

I CAN DO REACH & THROW RESCUES!

What else can I use?

Reach & Throw Rescues are fun but must be taken seriously to learn how to help in an emergency. In a real life event, I call the Emergency Services or find an adult to help. It is important I think carefully and keep myself safe at all times. Even good swimmers drown, so I do all I can by staying OUT of the water and not going in.

I use a Reach Rescue if the person having difficulty is close to the edge of the water. From the safety of the edge I can reach out with an item and rescue them – using things like sticks, palm fronds, broom handles, pool noodles, etc.

When I do a Reach Rescue, I check for danger before I approach then I call out to the person to get their attention and ask them to grab the item I am extending. I lay flat on the pool deck with only my arms out over the water and keep a very firm grip on the item I am extending to them. I stay low and flat on the ground to anchor myself and make sure I do not get pulled into the water as I pull the person towards me.

When I do a Throw Rescue, I always get the person in the water's attention and tell them what I am doing before I throw anything to them. As I throw, I anchor myself by kneeling or squatting to ensure I do not topple over or get pulled in. If the item I am throwing floats, I tell the person to either float with it and wait for help or kick back to safety. If the item I am throwing is a rope etc., I make sure I have a firm grip on it before I throw it and tell the person to grab it so I can pull them in safely.

REACH AND THROW DON'T GO!

MY ACHIEVEMENTS CHECKLIST

1 I get a little bit better each time I practise my swimming skills.

2 I record my progress using the checklist and a pencil.

3 It reminds me which skills I am really good at and which skills I will need to practise.

4 I know the more I practice the better I will get.

5 When I have practiced and perfected every skill, I know I am ready to move on to Level 4 of Learn to Swim The Australian Way.

Skill	Needs Work	Almost	Perfect
I can do a compact jump entry			
I can side breathe			
I can canoe float & kick			
I can missile float			
I can do angel wing swings			
I can backstroke march			
I can do rainbow arms			
I can do bubble arm breathing arm			
I can do a blast off on my back			
I can do a swordfish start & rotisserie roll			
I can mermaid underwater			
I can body dolphin			
I can do a torpedo streamline			
I can do six kicks lift & push			
I can do a frog legs sequence			
I can do a frog arms sequence			
I can do slow motion butterfly			
I can do underwater tumbles			
I can tread water & eggbeater kick			
I can do a crouch dive			
I can do reach & throw rescues			

CPSIA information can be obtained
at www.ICGtesting.com
Printed in the USA
BVHW062210160922
647217BV00003B/115